MW00398669

YHWH IS NOT A RADIO STATION IN MINNEAPOLIS

YHWH IS NOT A RADIO STATION IN MINNEAPOLIS
And Other Things Everyone Should Know

Written, Illustrated, and Choreographed
by
Craig McNair Wilson

1817

HARPER & ROW, PUBLISHERS, SAN FRANCISCO
Cambridge, Hagerstown, New York, Philadelphia
London, Mexico City, São Paulo, Sydney

FIRST EDITION

818
Wil

Designed by Catherine Flanders

Library of Congress Cataloging in Publication Data

Wilson, Craig McNair.
 YHWH is not a radio station in Minneapolis.

 1. Religion—Anecdotes, facetiae, satire, etc.
I. Title.   II. Title: Y. H. W. H. is not a radio station
in Minneapolis.
PN6231.R4W54   1983   818'.5402   82-48405
ISBN 0-06-069432-7

83 84 85 86 87 10 9 8 7 6 5 4 3 2 1

To my mom and dad,
who taught me to love God
and to ask everybody else
a lot of questions.

CONTENTS

They made me do it—write this book, I mean. It all started out as some late night doodlings in a long forgotten eatery. Here and there (but mostly Friday's, San Diego) more was added. One more gnarly aphorism scratched into a sketchbook. Three years and dozens of sketchbooks later it landed at Harper & Row San Francisco.

Along the way family, friends, and numerous waiters and waitresses have encouraged its completion. Mel and Lyla White (and of course Michael) read it and liked it—but only when it was good. The gang at the *Wittenburg Door* magazine saw pieces of it and knew, as I knew, that it would never go anywhere.

Its mood is part Bill Cosby, who taught us all good story telling; part Joe Bayly (and Herb Gooley), who showed me that Christian writing could be dazzling and not droll; and not just a little bit Ben Patterson, who made me be serious for a little bit—and introduced me to Frederick Buechner. And it's very much the bonfire of laughter that was a family meal when we'd tell stories of the silliness that churchianity can be.

My mother and father let me read, ask, consider anything. And find laughter in every moment. I did.

I always wanted to sneak into church some Saturday and rearrange the furniture. Then I'd mimeograph a new bulletin with the order of worship turned inside-out, adding the "Call to Laughter." Something to get folks to pay fresh attention.

The stories in this book, then, are not new, just some of the old ones turned inside-out.

I want you to like my book, sure, but more than that I want you to think about it. And laugh, but only when it's funny.

McNair
who would always rather be
in New York City eating
Chili at Charlie's, 45th Street

YHWH IS NOT A RADIO STATION IN MINNEAPOLIS

Adam

FIRST PERSON, FIRST LETTER. Adam was the first person to do just about everything: eat, talk, climb trees, and fall in love (see "E"). Adam was not the first person to use a Veg-o-matic. Adam was not unemployed. He was given a very important job. God asked Adam to give everything a name.

(Before Adam came along, God just pointed and said, "This thing here" or "That thing over there." And sometimes God would say, "No, not that one—the other one." And that's where all those sayings came from.)

So Adam sat on this rock, and when he saw something that he had never seen before, he would say, "This is a duck, that is a dog, this is a bush, and you are a sandwich!"

After several hours of naming things, Adam turned to someone near him and said, "Look, be an angel and get me something to drink."

And that's how angels were named.

BABEL

BABEL OR "BABBLE." In the Old Testament, Babel was a bunch of people who thought they could reach God by touching the sky. God didn't like their idea, so he confused them. And they didn't get any work done, and they didn't reach God.

Today a lot of people still babble. Some are understood, and some are not.

CAIN

THIRD LETTER AND THIRD PERSON. *Cain was the first son of Adam and Eve. But he was not always number one son. One day it was time for everyone to bring in their homework. Cain did the wrong assignment. Abel, his brother, did it right. God gave Abel an "A." Cain got an "F."*

When you're No. 2, you try harder. Sometimes you try too hard.

So . . . Cain killed Abel.

A RICH MAN TOLD JESUS, "Look. I have all this stuff: a beach house, a mountain cabin, cars, clothes, wine cellar, yacht, and a factory-direct-furniture warehouse."

This guy was shekels-up.

Then he asked, "Do you think I could get into heaven?"

His question seemed simple enough. Jesus' answer wasn't.

"Ha!" he laughed. "It would be easier for a camel to squeeze through a keyhole than for a rich man to get into Heaven."

And ever since then preachers, rich people, and especially rich preachers have argued about what Jesus meant. What do you think?

A. Rich people can't go to Heaven.
B. Camels can't go to Heaven.
C. Rich camels can't go to Heaven.
D. All keyholes in Heaven are small.

Children

WHO WE USED TO BE and wish we still were.

To get into some movies a child needs an adult guardian. To get into Heaven adults will need a child's heart. Or a child to vouch for them.

DANCE

SOME WALK, some stroll, some shuffle, some skip, some jog, some race, and some dance.

Children, artists, and angels dance.

Dance. It's the way God gets from place to place.

It's the way your body says, "I hear the music."

DEATH IS A DOOR with two sides. One side says "Exit" and
the other side says "Enter."

Epistle

THE BIBLE IS FULL OF LETTERS and letter writers. The most famous letter writer was Paul. He wrote letters and sent them all over the "known world." (That's what they used to call Asia Minor.)

Most of these letters were sent to famous churches in Ephesus, Galatia, Second Corinth, and other places. Paul never wrote to anybody in Dallas.

His most famous letter was written to the Italian Christians. In those days, most Italians lived in Rome (the capital city and the place where the main post office was). So Paul's letter to Italy was called "The Letter to All the Christians in and Around Rome and Their Friends."

To this day, a lot of Italians still live in Rome. They are called Romans. A lot of Italians do not live in Rome. They are just called Italians.

It's kind of like people who are Christians. Some go to church and some do not. The ones who go to church are called Christians. The ones who don't go are called absent.

Someday all Christians will be together with God in Heaven. Except those who are absent.

EVANGELISM

IT IS NOT SOMETHING YOU DO; it is something you are.
It's something you feel, not something you hear.
Evangelism is not noisy, but it is very loud.

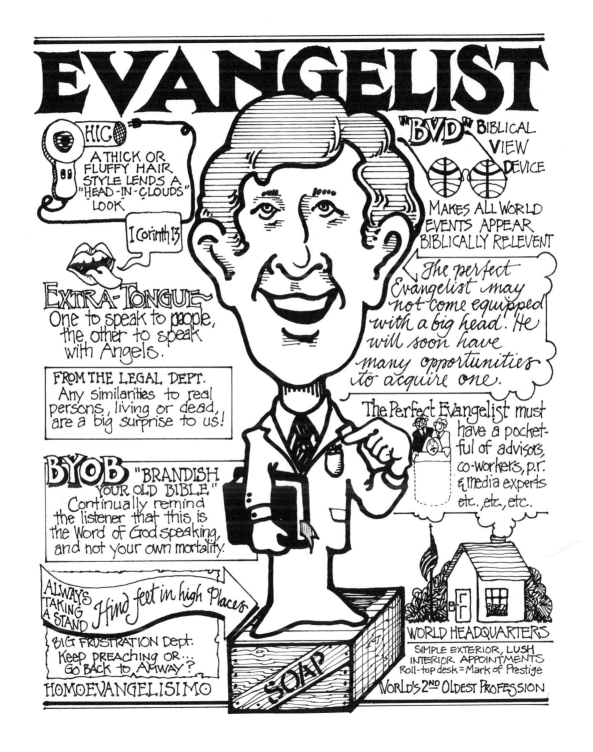

FISH

IT USED TO BE A SECRET SIGN to identify Christians. They don't have secret signs anymore. They have neon signs.

FORBIDDEN FRUIT

EUPHRATES GROWERS ASSOC.

THE VERY FIRST NEIGHBORHOOD anywhere was called Eden. It had everything you could ask for in a great neighborhood: flowers, vegetables, running water, beautiful lawns, waterfalls, pets, fruit trees, clear skies, sunshine, and underground utilities.

God asked Adam and Eve to live in Eden, enjoy themselves, have lots of kids, and "stay out of the banana grove!"

(There wasn't anything especially bad about bananas. God just wanted to see whether Adam and Eve would obey instructions or would decide for themselves what was good for them.)

One day Eve was taking an early morning walk when she met a banana salesman. They struck up a conversation, and before they knew it, it was lunchtime.

"Have you got any bananas here?" the salesman asked Eve.

"Oh. Why, yes," she said, "but God told us to stay away from the bananas and never eat them. Wouldn't you rather have a pomegranate or some granola?"

"No-o-o!" he roared, laughing at her. "I'm a banana man. If I don't have a couple of bananas every day, I'm just not myself."

"Oh." Eve said. She was worried. "But God said—"

"Horsefeathers!" The salesman's voice now thundered through Eden, shaking the trees. "God just said that because he knew that if you climbed up into those banana trees, you would be able to see the neighbor's garden—it's greener than Eden!"

"Neighbors?" Eve's curiosity was stirred. "I didn't know we had neighbors."

"Sure you do!" he continued. "And their garden is greener than Eden. God also knew that if you ate any bananas, you would be as smart as he is. Then he wouldn't be able to boss you around anymore!"

Eve was very confused, but what this guy was saying was very, very interesting to her. "You sure seem to know a lot about God and bananas."

"No kidding. I used to work for him. Why, I was his number one man. Then I discovered bananas, and God kicked me out of his organization. I was too smart for him!"

Well. Because Eve was curious about the neighbor's garden, and because they were very close to the banana grove and very hungry, and because Eve had tried all the other fruit in Eden, and because this salesman seemed very, very intelligent and seemed to know what he was talking about, they went to the banana grove. Eve got so excited when she tried her first banana that she forgot to climb up and look at the neighbor's garden. She just grabbed an armload of bananas and hurried home to tell Adam about the great new fruit.

When Eve told Adam about it, she did not roar like the salesman. She just grabbed the biggest banana in the bunch, peeled it very slowly, and took a great big bite. Then she smiled a great big smile and held the banana up to Adam's mouth . . . and . . . Adam smiled . . . and took a great big bite, too.

"Fantastic!" Adam announced with delight. What happened next was like a party. Adam and Eve began peeling and eating all of the bananas that Eve had brought home.

"WHAT'S GOING ON HERE?!"

A great big voice thundered like an earthquake through Eden. Adam and Eve knew it was God's voice, and that he was very mad. They dropped their bananas and started running for a place to hide. While they were running, they slipped and fell on all the empty banana peels.

And that's where God found them, lying among the banana peels. God told Eve and Adam that they would have to leave the garden of Eden because they had disobeyed him.

Today people are still slipping because they want to be as smart as God.

G is for gravy, which is never mentioned in the Bible

*"G" IS ALSO FOR GOD. He is mentioned in the Bible. A lot.
I think you already knew that.*

EVERYBODY WANTS TO GO THERE, but nobody wants to buy a ticket.

SOME PEOPLE BELIEVE IN HELL. Some people don't. Someday they will.

Once upon a time

It all started with

the first thing that happened was

To begin with on the very first day At the start of

the beginning was

At the beginning

In

In the beginning

~~In the beginning~~

IN THE BEGINNING

WHEN GOD—WHO LIVED "IN THE BEGINNING"—decided to get it all going, Moses, an old friend, suggested that they should write some of it down. "So we won't forget it," Moses explained.

"That's a great idea, Moses. Why don't you do that?"

Moses was not a very good talker, but as it turned out, he was a pretty good writer.

To get him started, God gave Moses a few notes from the beginning—since Moses was not "in the beginning."

From: God
To: Moishé
Re: In the beginning

It all started with what seemed like a pretty good idea at the time: spheres of color and light swirling thru space (we had a lot of space back then) with a deep blue background. A little gas, a few minerals, ~~several barrels~~ of water and ~~truckloads~~ tons of dirt. (Dirt was a wonderful development.) We all took a week off to work on it. And it worked great! The first thing we did was light — lots of light — so we could see what we were doing and so we didn't put everything in the same place and so everything wouldn't ~~get~~ bump into each other. Light was good. (Light may be my favorite thing, except for children.)

We made thousands of animals next. (Botanists and zoologists were developed later to explain it all.)

(Now when I say "good" I mean it worked.)

As for how much time it ~~the~~ took us to do all of this, it's not important. What is important is that we <u>did</u> it.

Finally we made man. No, I mean people. No— I mean man. That was good! Then we made woman. That was good too— in some ways woman was better.

Man and woman hit it off pretty well right from the start. (They had very similar tastes.)

___

That should cover the first chapter, Mo. We can fill in the details later. When we were finished we sat around for a day or so and just enjoyed it!

G.

P.S. I hope you can read this —English was not my first language.

"I start with two Galilean trout. If you are serving more than 10,000, just double everything."

JOHN WAS THE COUSIN OF JESUS. John's father was a priest, but John became a preacher anyway. His headquarters was in a wilderness area outside the city—waterfront property. John did not preach in a church. He was an "evangelist" (do not see "E").

John did not have his own t.v. show. His favorite saying was, "Hey! Watch out, 'cause God is coming!"

His favorite outdoor sport was dunking people in the Jordan River. The people who were dunked wanted to show everybody that they were changing their lives (see "U"). Dunking meant an end to the old, bad life and the beginning of a new life.

Because of all this dunking, John was given a nick-name. He was called John the Dunker.

(Ever since then, people have used his name for all kinds of religious organizations: the Southern Dunkers Convention, the First Dunken Church, the General Association of Regular Dunkers, Dunkers General Conference, Swedish Dunkers, American Dunkers, and Dunkin' Doughnuts.)

A lot of people are still getting dunked today. Some dunk their whole bodies underwater using a lake, an ocean, or a swimming pool. Some churches even have a built-in dunkistry.

Others just sprinkle a little water on their heads, splash behind the ears, dab a drop here and there on special trouble spots, or give themselves a thorough hose-down. How and where it happens is not important.

When we get to Heaven, St. Peter won't be checking for water marks. Promise.

NOT EVERYONE who kisses you is your friend.

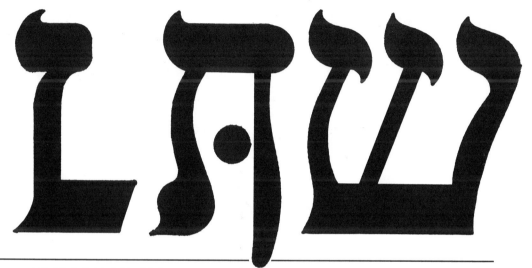

THE LAW OF GOD IS PERFECTION.

Why does God have to be so strict?

In a football game, you have to get the ball over the goal line to score a touchdown. Maybe it should be enough if you play fairly well and get the ball near the line. Why do you always have to get the ball over the line?

A loving God would be that way. Anybody who has been pretty good or near good or sort of good . . . picky, picky, picky.

A LEPER IS SOMEONE with a very bad sickness. It used to be that if you were a leper, you couldn't live in a regular house. Lepers lived in special neighborhoods outside big cities.

Today not only lepers, but other people as well, are kept out of neighborhoods. They are kept out because they are different. Because they are brown or crippled or mentally retarded.

But the people who keep them out have a sickness worse than leprosy. They have ignorance. And it's very, very contagious.

MICAH

PROPHET OF GOD.

The Bible is full of stories about prophets and what they said. Most of the time, it was not good news.

Micah worked at Doom & Gloom, Inc. Like his friend Isaiah, he didn't even want the job. Being a prophet is no fun.

That was the old days.

Today there are prophets, too.

The prophets today are not anything like Micah. These new prophets seem to enjoy saying scary, terrible things. And they write lots of books, instead of following the old way of just speaking one message and then going back to their jobs as night managers at 7-11.

Jesus said that someday many will speak in God's name, but not be sent from him. They are called false prophets.

If you ever meet someone on the street or hear someone on television who says he or she is a prophet—sent from God—just listen very closely to everything that person says. If the message is different from what God tells us in the Bible, then you have probably met a false prophet—maybe even a banana salesman.

MOSES

LEADER OF HIS PEOPLE, ex-shepherd, ex-leader of someone else's people.

Moses found out that a career shift late in life isn't such a bad thing.

THE BUILDING BLOCK OF LIFE.

It is mud that God rolled around in his hand and used to make Adam.

Later Jesus used some mud (following an old family recipe that called for dirt and saliva) to make Blind Bartimaeus 20/20.

With all the mud around everywhere, it's a wonder that only God has found a good use for it.

nationality

THE BIBLE HAS LOTS OF NUMBERS IN IT: 12 tribes; 6 days of creation; 10 commandments; 9 lepers; 5 loaves of bread and 2 Galilean rainbow trout; 12 baskets full; 2 thieves; 1 great big fish; 7 (trained) seals; and 969 years (the age of the oldest person in history—so far). Some of its numbers are so big that only words like multitude *can be used. The Bible has a "multitude" of heavenly hosts.*

But the highest number in the Bible started when God promised Abraham that he would be the father with the most children.

That was how the nation of Israel began. Abraham's children were the Children of God. Now everyone who chooses to follow Jesus becomes a child of God—and Abraham.

So how many children does Abraham have? They're still counting.

ORIGINAL SIN

SOME PEOPLE WILL TELL YOU that original sin was what happened in the garden when Adam and Eve disobeyed God and ate the forbidden fruit (see "F").

Original sin means you did it. You will be judged for what you did—not for what your parents did. It isn't Adam's fault, or the month you were born.

It's all yours—you did it.

And I'm telling.

Prayer

CONVERSATION. SOUNDS EASY. Most of us tend to forget that conversation means listening as well as talking. Usually, when we think about prayer, we think about praying to God.

You can pray anywhere. Inside or outside. In the dark, on the run, at a movie, underwater, with a friend, or even in a church basement. You can even pray at school—whenever you want to.

A lot of folks pray at bedtime. Like when your mom used to say, "Brush your teeth, turn off the lights, say your prayers, and turn off your stereo."

Sometimes we pray before we eat. (Except at McDonald's. There you just scratch your head and say, "Thanks, God.")

Usually, though, we pray when we want something or when we are in pain (see "Y").

Sometimes we pray when we don't know what else to do and can't even think of what to say to God. Maybe we are lonely. But lonely is a word. Which means that somebody has already felt this way before and made up a name for the feeling. Only we want it to be our own special and private problem. We do not want to call our feeling what everyone else has called it.

So we make up our own name for our problem. Our

very own, brand-new, never-before-spoken language. Like, "AUGH!" or "Y-R-R-B!" or even "F-DL-TH-TH-M!"

That's okay, because God speaks all languages: American, Urdu, Swahili, Mexican, French, Amheric, Baby-talk, Japanese, Mung, Gaelic, Braille, Jive, Southern Methodist, and Elfan. God even understands Seminary Professor.

No matter which language you use to talk, sing, whisper, think, or yell to God, he listens. And he answers. Always.

Don't forget to listen.

PREACHER!

"MY SERMON THIS MORNING is from the second chapter of my new book. Copies are available at the back. Now let us close in prayer. 'Our father . . .'"

QUICK

AS IN FAST. Right now! And, "That wasn't there a minute ago."

The Bible tells about special messengers from God— angels. On only a few occasions does the Bible tell us their names: Michael, Gabriel, Ariel, Low ("and Low, the Angel of the Lord, came upon them," Luke 2), and Suddenly ("Suddenly, the Angel of God, was in their midst," Acts 12).

Seems like in the Bible nothing happens slowly.

REVO

JESUS SAID WHEN SOMEONE HURTS US we should "turn the other cheek." Most of us wish it was the other guy's cheek.

RIVER

A LOT OF STUFF IN THE BIBLE *happens in, near, or through rivers. In fact, if you include lakes and oceans and wells, well then, we'd have to say that water is a pretty important part of the Bible. (And leave us not forget rain and flood.)*

One of the most interesting "rivermen" in the Bible—other than John (see "J")—was Naaman (pronounced Naymun).

Naaman was very, very rich. He was also very, very sick. You could see the sores all over his body.

In the midst of all of his coughing and groaning, Naaman got a message from God. It was delivered by the neighborhood prophet (see "M"). In the message, God told Naaman that the only way he could get rid of his sickness was to go down to the River Jordan and get completely underwater.

Naaman knew that the Jordan was a dirty river so he wanted to just sprinkle a little water on his head. "Kind of a symbolic washing," Naaman insisted.

God suggested that if he wanted to get completely well, he would have to get completely wet.

"In fact," God said, "Why don't you go down seven times!" (You see, seven is God's lucky number.)

After a lot of discussion back and forth, Naaman went down for the seven count.

And it worked! Every last one of Naaman's ugly old sores had completely vanished (see "V").

Now, even though a lot of folks have heard this story, they still don't want to get into God's way of doing things: *completely*.

Rock Star

"THIS NEXT SONG ISN'T VERY SPECIAL to me, the Lord didn't write it, the words are kinda shallow and meaningless, but it's got a great beat, almost as good as the Bee Gees' song it's copied after. Dig? Dig."

SNAKE

THE STORY GOES that a snake handed a lady some fruit, and next thing she knew she was in a lot of trouble. Ever since then, snakes have not had hands or been allowed to talk.

TEN COMMANDMENTS

SOME PEOPLE DON'T LIKE THE TEN COMMANDMENTS, but for a movie that was made back in 1956, you'll have to admit it was very impressive.

In one of the big scenes, Moses (played by Charlton Heston with a lot of white hair and a very interested look on his face) goes up a mountain to see God.

What he finds is a bush that is burning, but doesn't get burned up! That would put an interested look on anybody's face.

The bush also talks. Really, it's God's voice. Well really, it's Charlton Heston's voice. (Maybe that was cheaper than getting another actor. Maybe Orson Wells was out of town. Or maybe that's how God really sounds to some people— just like themselves. Who's going to remember what the voice sounded like?)

It is what the voice said *that's* important.

That was about three thousand years ago. Today we have thousands of laws to help us remember what that voice told Moses, but they all boil down to two things: love God completely and don't hurt anybody.

THOMAS

IF HE WERE ALIVE TODAY, Doubting Thomas would live in Missouri. His favorite phrases were, "Oh yah?" and, "Really?" and, "You're kiddin'!"

Some folks will believe anything they hear. Not Thomas.

He wanted a second opinion. He wanted to hear it from a more reliable source. Thomas also said, "Seeing is believing."

When Thomas finally saw Jesus—after the resurrection—Jesus said, "Not seeing, yet believing—that's believing!"

UNDER NEW MANAGEMENT

SOMETIMES PEOPLE who own bicycle shops and gas stations decide to move to another town and sell caramel corn. Before they move, they sell their store to a new owner. The people put a sign in the window that says, "Under New Management."

The store still sells bicycles or gasoline, but the new owners always make improvements. Same store, only better.

When people become Christians, they are still the same people—same personalities, but with a few changes—for improvement.

Now they are "under new management."

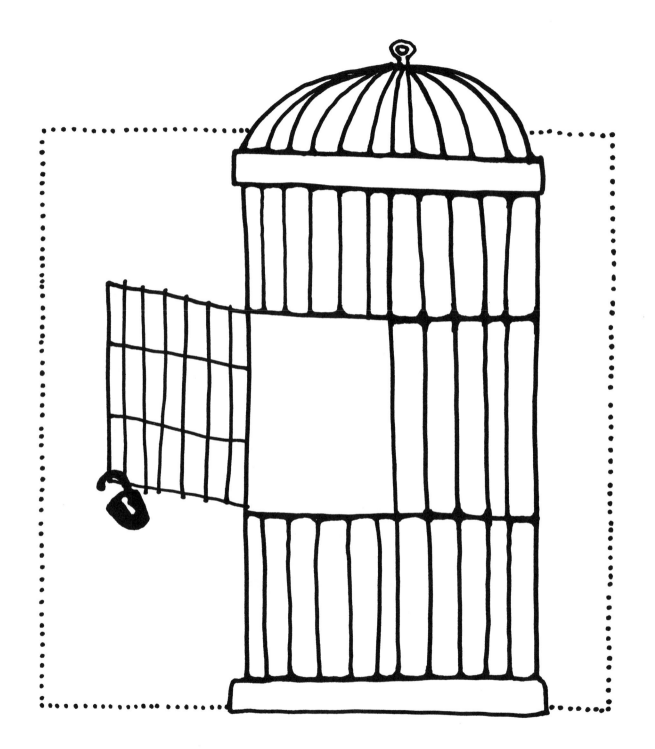

VANISH IS THE PLACE where our sins go when we give them to God.

Wine

"Yes, the Christian Brothers Cabernet
will be just fine."

WISEMAN

A WISEMAN WAS A KING from the East (Ethiopia, Babylon, and Persia, but not Ohio). A bunch of them came to see the newest and best king ever—Jesus.

It took them a long, long time to get to Jesus' house. They found his house by following a great light for more than a year.

Most people think that there were only three wisemen. There were probably fourteen—at least. We just say that there were only three so they will all fit on our coffee tables at Christmas.

ABOUT THE ONLY TIME you hear about "X" anymore is at Xmas time. That is when the whole world celebrates the birth of Baby X. Some people don't like it when you say "Xmas." They think that the big X is to cross out the word Christ.

What really happened was that a Greek delicatessen was having a big Christmas party. They wanted to invite everyone. It was decided that a large sign saying "CHRISTMAS PARTY" would be made and placed in the window of the deli.

As it happened, they had only one window and it was very small. They knew, though, that in the Greek language the symbol for the name of Christ is X.

So they made a sign that said, "Xmas Party." Not only did it fit in their small shop window, but the sign was also very catchy.

Soon Xmas signs could be seen everywhere—even though a lot of shopkeepers didn't know that X means "Christ."

Many Xians (followers of X) got very upset. Some of them even made signs protesting: "KEEP CHRIST IN CHRISTMAS."

But he was. Always had been and always will be.

YHWH

YHWH IS NOT A RADIO STATION IN MINNEAPOLIS. *It is the name of God. He also answers to "friend," "king," "father," "Lord," and most often "Help!"*

The Jews believed God's name should not be said aloud, so they wrote it in a way that couldn't be spoken. Later, YHWH became Jehovah, and eventually Lord.

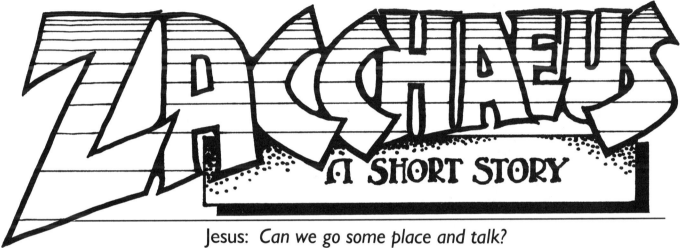

ZACCHAEUS

A SHORT STORY

Jesus: *Can we go some place and talk?*

Zacch: *Your place or mine?*

Jesus: *Better be yours. I don't have a place.*

Zacch: *What do you like to drink?*

Jesus: *Do you have any Constant Comment?*

Zacch: *So I'm told. (Pause.)*
        What's it like being the Son of God?

Jesus: *What's it like being short?*

SOMEONE WHO IS VERY EXCITED about a cause, an idea, or a belief. Zealots are really "into it." If you've read this far, you are a zealot. You are into it.